T0369057

Reflections from Beyond

A Book of Wisdom

By William deGraftColeman

iUniverse, Inc.
Bloomington

Reflections from Beyond
A Book of Wisdom

This is a work of intuition, and of a personal journey. Any reference to any work or person is purely coincidental.

Scripture quotations marked NLT are from the New Living Translation, copyright 1996, Used by permission of the following publishers:

Tyndale House Publishers, Inc., Weaton, Illinios 60189. All rights reserved.

iUniverse books may be ordered through booksellers or by contacting:

iUniverse
1663 Liberty Drive
Bloomington, IN 47403
www.iuniverse.com
1-800-Authors (1-800-288-4677)

ISBN: 978-1-4620-2854-2 (sc)
ISBN: 978-1-4620-2855-9 (hc)
ISBN: 978-1-4620-2856-6 (e)

Library of Congress Control Number: 2011931367

Printed in the United States of America

iUniverse rev. date: 08/02/2011

To my family and friends.

Acknowledgement

I would like to express my heartfelt gratitude to the Almighty God for the miracle that splintered my world of darkness with rays of light; and Doctor Pouc Huu Pham[x] for his high level of professionalism and dedication for handling my condition the best way possible. My deep appreciation also goes to Lucinda Basset's Midwest Center for Stress and Anxiety[x] for sharing an invaluable resource with me; and my pastors, Sylvester Athoro of House of Glory Church[x], and Bishop Dr. Akotua Obeng of Liberty Evangelical Bible Ministries[x] for their in- depth teachings and prayers.

Last but not the least is Kwesi Korreh,[x] Barrister at Law, Florida and New Jersey, for his profound support in making sure this work sees the light of day.

x- Additional information provided on last page.

When a man exhibits favor to his fellowman, he exhibits the flavor in humanity.

Introduction

My Story

"*Do for others what you would like them to do for you...*" *So says a valuable verse in the Holy Book regarding relationships among men on Earth. Mathew 7:12 NLT.*

I am a middle aged man of forty-two years, a trained journalist and author of the fascinating novel The Gods Declare.[x] For over twenty years, I could say, I was practically non-functional as I suffered what my doctor, Phouc Huu Pham, of Orlando, Florida, and Angela Basset's Midwest Center for Stress and Anxiety diagnosed, and confirmed as severe Anxiety and Panic Disorder. So debilitating and destructive this condition was that not a single day passed without the thought of suicide re-echoing in my mind.

I was reclusive and cloaked in fear, and for over twenty years I harbored my anguish all within. I had no friends, couldn't handle any job, and lacking the courage to open up to my family, I suffered a great deal of loneliness as a consequence. Like a caged pet, I looked on helplessly as my peers soared passed me in every field of human endeavor.

Stepping out of the door was like stepping into a trap. I lived only in my mind and with the mere break of dawn sending shivers down my spine I withdrew even deeper into myself. On occasions that I ventured out, I had to rely on the generosity of others for the simplest of chores although I am not physically disabled.

I came upon the above quote one gloomy day when a well accoutered lady who was struggling writing in front of a banker asked for my help. Knowing I couldn't because of my condition, I whirled around with embarrassment only to bump into another lady distributing gospel tracts. This woman handed me one with the quote and after a momentary reflection turned back to assist the lady. I struggled with nervousness whilst writing but in the end I realized I had helped her. I realized I had not only fulfilled a deep – seated wish of helping others but that I had also obeyed a biblical commandment.

That event which I believe deeply was a miracle marked the beginning of my transformation, a spiritual transformation so to speak, I took the scripture leaflet home and in the dark cold corner of my room began studying the Holy Book. Something strange, something indescribable began to happen as I flipped through page after page the Book of Proverbs and Psalms reflecting and meditating. I realized for the first time in my life that a door had literary been opened through which I saw my condition and in fact everything around me in a completely different perspective giving me an incomparable solace. Suddenly, I realized the immense imagination I am endowed with together with an insight I never knew existed.

Overtime, I developed a ritual of prayer and meditation every morning, and on each occasion, these quotes and thoughts gathered in this book, and many more will flood my mind like impounded water from a broken levee. Instead of being overshadowed by fear and panic, I would visualize these negative feelings as entities and then derive a positive quote or thought to dispel them. When I am down and out, I will go through this exercise and then come up with a quote about hope in other to uplift my soul. So enriching and fulfilling was this practice that it became a therapy for me. Eventually I began to scribble here and scribble there.

Later, I began a compilation on the advice of my pastor and spiritual counselor. I took this step not only to inspire those like me but most especially, I took this step to share these insights in a broader context because I realized that today, in our world, strife abounds everywhere you turn; in our homes, in our neighborhoods and communities, and in distant lands.

From dawn to dusk, and from one revolution of the Earth to another, peace abounds yet peace eludes man. Like an evasive goal, man struggles at peace but momentarily. The solution seems farfetched, even improbable to some. But if all or even some would pause to reflect deeply on the quote above, a greater burden, a burden that has impeded the collective progress of man could not forever remain insurmountable.

Man is frail both in nature and in substance, but man has erroneously ignored this and championed a life of total independence and self – worth. Despite countless examples, one of which has been cited above, proving that a man's survival is contingent on others, however insignificant, man is sadly blinded.

Life is worthy, life is precious, but this can be realized to the full when man recognizes that he is an embodiment of his fellowman irrespective of his social standing and or health.

This is the purpose of the book; to serve as a reminder to sufferers and the healthy alike that all is not lost, that the Creator, or Nature or whatever it is that you believe in imbedded in us the power to make life worth living.

Please, as you reflect, and meditate on the contents, let your thoughts and enlightenment radiate in practical ways: extend a helping hand to the needy when it is in your capacity to do so. Be humane not only to yourself but to humanity in general and in so doing, you will not only encounter an inner peace, but one that would extend to others in ways you can never imagine.

Thanks.

Author's note:

Reflections From Beyond is in two parts. Part one are quotes and thoughts derived as a result of the Author's attempt in understanding and countering fear, and hopelessness.

Part two are quotes and insights focusing generally on the essence of the Creator, of man, and the relationship among men.

Part One

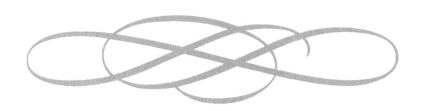

Fear

unchecked is like a beast untamed.

If inspiration were glass, many would stare.

Faith in God helps us to control our anxieties, but our anxieties uncontrolled could make us lose faith in God!

The Peace of God fills us with the hope that one day all of our woes would come to an end, but an unfounded belief could never end our woes.

Faith

is fortified not by

fear

but

by

faith!

*The only benefit
derivative from
fear is when it is focused
on the Creator,
any other thing is an illusion.*

No matter

how severe your

*trials are, they pale in comparison
in severity to that of the Christ!*

Do not be

deceived in believing

you are the owner of your own life,
for in reality you are owned!

A man may

treasure his wealth by all measure,
but the Fear of the

Lord is a treasure beyond every
measure.

A Man

may picture a particular setting for

his life, but without the Grace of that

which Dwells

Within, and hard work, the

setting could forever remain

a

picture.

*Though
man's efforts
at perfection is relative,
God's perfection
is
a
relationship.*

When

you balk

at fear,

your

bulk would be nothing but

frail.

To
dump your fears, you
must
leap in
faith!

The

fuel for

a Man's

life

is not

his

fears

but his

courage.

Why lose

sleep pondering how to be perfect,
rather let your imperfections be
buried in your sleep.

If you

spend your life looking up to the heavens, your vision for your life would be blurred.

Fear

shrinks a man but courage springs him.

If you
pray without fear, fear can never
prey on

you.

When you

*draw close to the Creator, you
draw strength, but when you
withdraw from Him, you*

draw fear.

A soothing

voice commands attention, but a booming one commands

fear!

It is

*better to crave for the fear of God
than to cave in to the fear of man.*

The exercise of one's faith is like swimming; some take a leap, others dip.

If you

dwell on what scares you, what scares you will dwell

on you.

End of Part One.

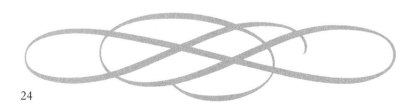

Part two

A word of

wisdom is like a meal that satisfies but a few!

If you stay

tuned by wisdom, your life will be fine-tuned by

wisdom!

When a man

extends courtesy to his fellowman,
he exhibits the commonality in

humanity.

Every

random act of kindness is rewarded with a deliberate act

of blessing.

Since creation,

greed remains the single most dreaded plague ever to befall the

human race.

Man is

nothing but a speck of dust; know this and share

this and share

your wealth!

Though precise
mathematical laws governs the
universe, relationships among men
need not be governed by

mathematics.

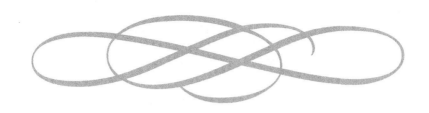

Love

is like a fetus : It's amazing in origin yet frail in

nature.

True peace

is attained not by loving your enemies; true peace is attained by being wary of

your friends.

Ever wondered
why you can't
determine your own path?
Consider this: You are
Predetermined!

*When a
man nurtures his fellowman, he is
himself nurtured by

nature.*

The pursuit

*of happiness is like the search
of a needle in a hay stack: It
requires diligence, hard work, and
sometimes luck.*

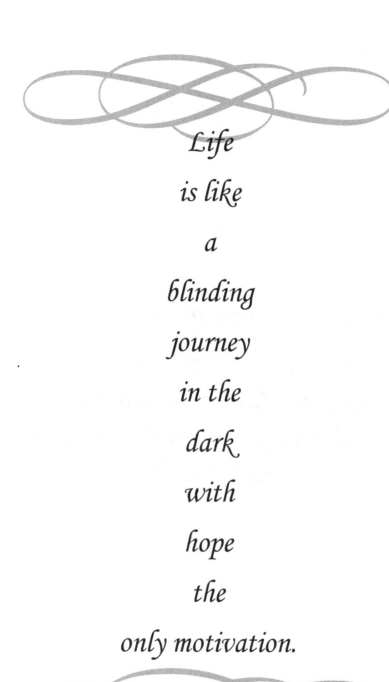

Life

is like

a

blinding

journey

in the

dark

with

hope

the

only motivation.

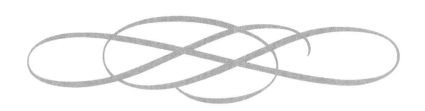

The world
might be full
of mysteries
but the
greatest mystery
ever to confound man
is man himself.

A man's security

is

provided not by

latches and locks,

but by the

love that

exceeds the human

comprehension.

To

acknowledge

your imperfections

is to appreciate

your very humanity,

but to decline is to

deny your very

essence!

Sympathy
is like a
language
spoken
by many,
but understood
by few!

The measure
of a man does not
lie in his
attainment of
laurels, but in his
ability to co-exist
with his fellowman.

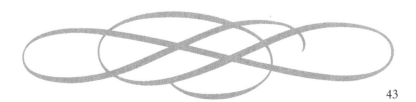

The

complexity

of man

is

the miniature

of God

manifest!

*If wisdom was
imbibed to the largest
of creatures, the tiniest
would be the most
unwise!*

Jealousy and
vengeance
are two sides
of the same coin but, love and
compassion mirrors each
other.

If judgment

is

by appearance,

courtrooms

would be

fashion houses.

*A man
with no self-control is
like a
vessel
without
controls!*

To
perceive
words of wisdom,
one must do
one thing:
Listen!

Do not rejoice
in a fool's prosperity,
rather be glad in
the company of the wise!

If a man's dwellings

*were the judge of his character,
the wealthy would*

be the most righteous!

Consolation

is like

a string;

it

binds

humanity

agelessly.

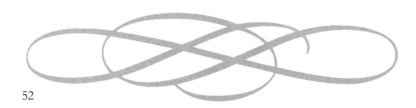

Instead

of timing your adversaries into disaster,

let your counsel be

a timely intervention!

Every day as you breath,

seek not for a better life;

rather strive to

avoid a

bitter end.

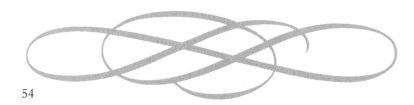

Do not be bothered

by

the words

of the enemy,

rather be bothered by

his fate.

As perseverance
is the
preserve of
the wise,
so is laziness
the preference
of the fool.

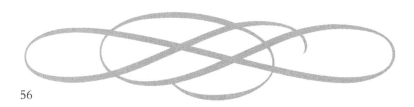

Ever wondered why you can't

pull your

weight?

Consider

pushing your

way.

If

you

focus on

the cup, you

can

overcome every

handicap.

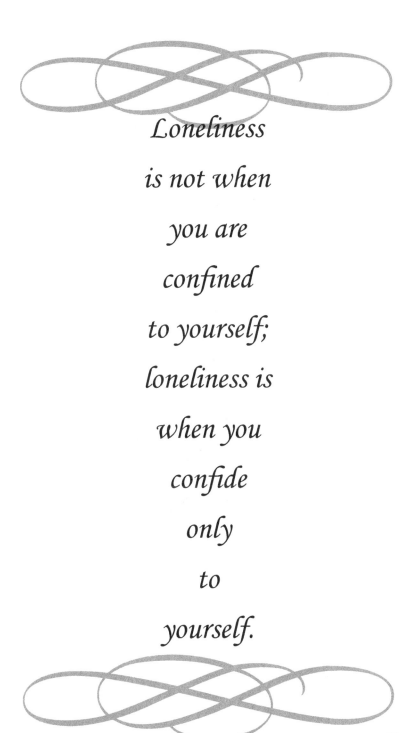

Loneliness
is not when
you are
confined
to yourself;
loneliness is
when you
confide
only
to
yourself.

It is a proof
you have your
head
when
you
have a roof
over your
head.

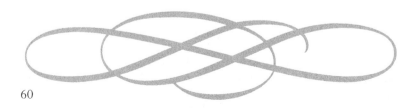

Being
right does not make
you wise;
being
wise makes you
right.

If you
are disposed to
rage;
you are
a disposal for
rage.

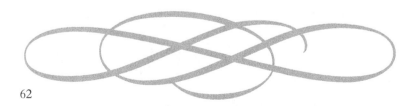

The

greatest

expenditure

a man

could ever incur

is when

he helps

his fellowman at his

own

expense.

*A man
who conquers at
war is a conqueror, but a man
who concurs for the sake of
war conquers all.*

No matter
how big his appetite,
the
soul of
the foodie is always
famished.

Since

creation,

greed remains the

single most driving force

against universal equity.

If economic
privileges were to guarantee
peace,
only the poor would be
at
war!

Since ages,
man's imperfection
continues to remain the only
commonality
among men.

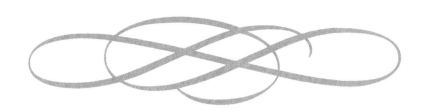

The

power

in humility

is the

honor

in

nobility.

Immunity
to fellow feeling
is nothing but impunity to
all of humanity.

*Though education
is the key to many
doors,
the door to that which Dwells
Within requires
no key!*

*If the
human thought were to
be audible,
the world as we know would
be
uninhabitable.*

"If each man
will be still in other
to examine his attitudes,
life as we know would
come to a standstill."

Since creation,

it is the heart

and not the law that remains

the single most

powerful

tool in

the

fight against

hatred.

The reason

man

was made a

gregarious

being was to

demonstrate the commonality

among

men.

The most
powerful influence ever
to
impact
man
is man
himself.

To

be

sympathetic

is to be

humane,

but to be empathetic is a

Godly trait!

Let not

your life be a balancing act,

instead

let your life be in

balance with that which

Dwells Within.

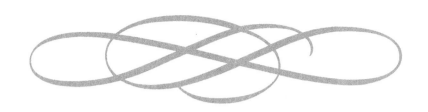

*Let not your
mental powers clout
your vision, rather let your
mental powers be your
vision.*

In everything,
seek not to justify your
every action, instead let your
actions be your every
justification.

Instead

of being hard-hearted towards others,

be warmhearted

towards the downhearted.

People
who mistreat
others most often end
up being maltreated
by their
very own.

A modest

lifestyle is pleasant to the eye, but a lifestyle of opulence

is an

eyesore.

*If life
is about competition,
sportsmen would be
Rulers.*

*A man
may fortify himself within
his walls, but the protection of
that Which Dwells within needs
no
fortification.*

Integrity

is like

a garment

worn

only by

a

few.

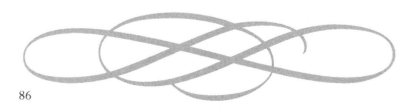

The goal of mankind
is to attain self-
dependence, but the goal of that
which abides Within is to attain
man's dependence.

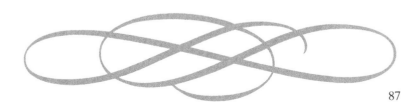

A man

full of airs is nothing

but

a man

filled

with errs!

*A man
who boasts about his
guts is nothing but a
weakling
in the
gut!*

When a person
places his hope in his wealth,
he places an order for his
wreath!

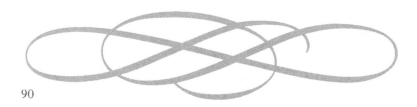

It is

not

old age that stoops a

man, rather

heavy-heartedness stoops

a man

irrespective of age.

*When
hope is
deferred, life is denied,
and when life is denied, hope
is
defeated.*

*If laws
were made only for the
wise,
fools would
be
rulers!*

Arrogance
is like a walk
stick
aiding
only the
fool!

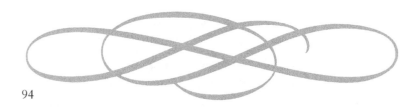

Taking advantage of your fellowman only

makes a mockery of

your very

essence.

Stupidity

is a

condition perceived

only by

the

wise!

*When a
man joins the hand of
another, there is harmony, but
when the hand is disengaged, strife
is embraced.*

*It is
better to share your
weight
than to
shed your
weight!*

A
captain
isn't a man
with a cap,
a captain is
a man with
a cup.

Ever

wondered what the future

holds?

Consider the wonders held

by nature.

When you
cavort with a fool,
you are branded a fool, but when
you
associate with
the wise,
wisdom
becomes
your brand.

If you

want

your life to be straight,

strive to

be straightforward!

*As a
man's desire for knowledge
is unending, so is the knowledge of the
Creator without end.*

A Man who

holds negative

perception indefinitely is nothing
but a troubled man by

definition.

*If you
look high on yourself,
you are probably
too high to be noble.*

A man

who keeps his mouth shut is a secret keeper, but one who doesn't is the messenger of

trouble!

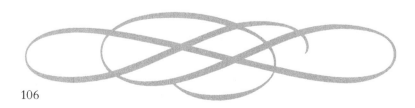

*A Good
name isn't better
than riches;
a good
name is
wealth!*

*Too much
pleasure can lead to poverty,
but too much poverty
is no
pleasure either.*

*It is
safer to be kissed by an
enemy than to be accused by
a friend.*

In making

life choices,

the wise probes beneath the

surface, but for the fool, the surface is the

horizon.

Until man

visualizes himself in another,
marginalization

would never

cease to

exist.

Secular
living is nothing but
circular reasoning for
living.

In
life, every
positive step is a
building block, but every step not
taken is a
block undone.

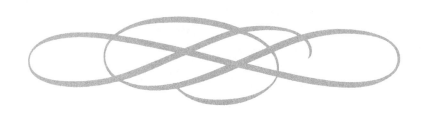

Though mankind is a
minute part of the
vast universe,
his role
in the
universe is
anything but
minute.

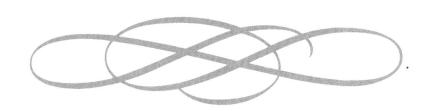

If you
doze throughout your life,
you will be bulldozed throughout
your life.

A man
full of
pomp is
like a
pump full
of air!

It is
one thing being wounded
in the flesh, and being wounded
in the spirit quite
another.

Lack of knowledge
is like a
snare;
It leaves
no spare!

Every

man is

an envoy

in the

human

employ.

The

greatest

possession a man

could ever own isn't his

wealth; it is

his word!

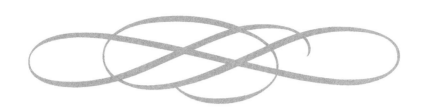

A
kind gesture is a
Divine Inspiration
but the desire to
sacrifice is a Divine
Intervention!

*Until
man has a firm grasp of
his essence,
he will
continue to gasp at
his very essence!*

Though
God
the Creator
is invincible,
His every creation
makes Him
abundantly visible!

Willing
obedience
is fruitful than
a grudging one!

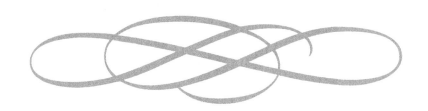

To be stable,
one needs to be sturdy,
but to be sturdy, one needs to
be strong.

Though,

scanning the universe takes the breath away,

knowledge of that which Dwells Within is breathtaking beyond compare!

*The pathway
of life is like a
highway to
only one
destination:
salvation
or destruction.*

Pleasant
words
bears
goodness,
but
words from
the evil-
hearted
is always cloaked with malice.

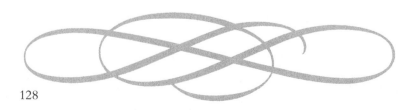

Ever found
life hard to cope?
Consider holding out
hope!

Life isn't about
being hard-hearted;
life is
about lending
your hard hat
to the vulnerable.

It is one

thing getting away

with a crime, and walking away
from a crime quite another.

The best

motivation

a man could ever render, is the recognition of

himself in his

fellowman.

Until man

recognizes love as his pre-eminent
quality,

man's quality of life
would forever be devoid

of

affection.

The
greatest error
a man could
ever make is
fearing he
will commit
one.

If you
believe
in anything,
you have no price, but if you
believe in yourself,
you are priceless!

If the dead

were

powerful,

the living

would

wish to be dead.

The
day
each man
stands by his word,
all strife
would
end.

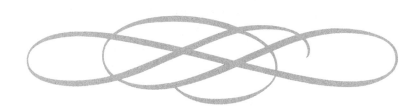

Do

not

prey

on

others,

instead

pray

for

others.

*It is
better to
be mildly
tempered than to be
wildly
mannered.*

The
world
abounds
in wisdom
yet
wisdom
eludes
the world.

*Light
and
darkness are distinct
in nature
yet complimentary in
in every way.*

Purity
of the heart is Godliness in
the heart!

Humility and
pride are
no
bedfellows,
likewise
bravery
and
cowardice.

In

the

beginning

was a Vision,

and the

Vision was

from God,

and the

Vision

was Man.

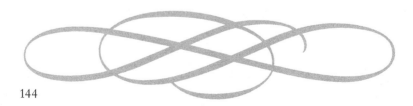

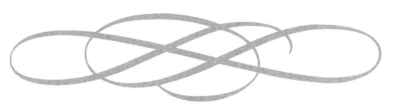

The

Earth was

created

out of

nothing

but man was

created

out of

something :

God!

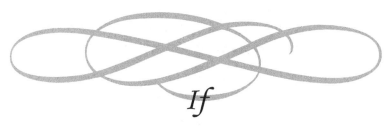

If

you

believe there

are no

miracles

in

the world

today,

witness a

childbirth

today!

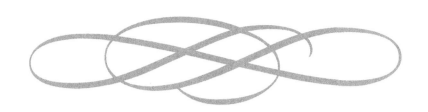

To make

life

meaningful,

do only

one

thing:

Breath!

God

made man

in

His own

Image so

man

would

reflect

his nature.

When you

reflect on

how you

were

made,

you would

live in awe

of the One

who made

you!

Though
the gift of freewill is dignifying,
its application is
nothing close.

*If
you really want
to experience the
spiritual realm,
focus on spirituality.*

The

mind

is the

sole connection to the other side,

lose it and you are stuck on

this side!

Rather
than letting
your
assets become a
liability,
let your
liabilities
be your
assets.

*A man
with no
belief system is like a
mobile sewage system;
only sludge fuels
his existence.*

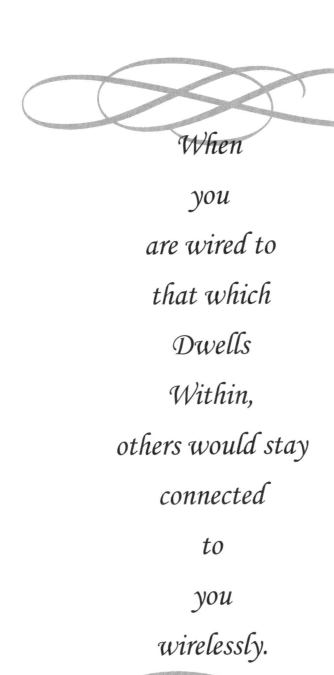

When

you

are wired to

that which

Dwells

Within,

others would stay

connected

to

you

wirelessly.

Not

reaching

your goal

is not

as

hopeless

as not

having

one.

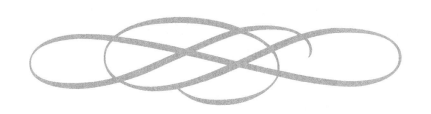

Awareness

of one's self is not enough;
awareness of one's nature

is more

than

enough.

*If you don't
know your place,
others
would take your place.*

Sounding one's
own horn is like a melodious music fit
only for the hearing
impaired!

*If you
equate happiness with materialism,
your life would be nothing but an
equation for*

commercialism.

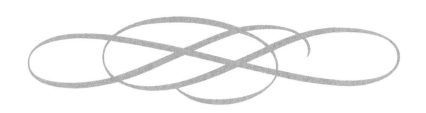

Rather

than

carrying a banner espousing your manners,

let

your manners be

your banner.

Materialism

is costly and does not ensure life:
Spirituality

isn't but ensures

life

abundantly.

The reason

life

is increasingly becoming

unbearable

is because attitudes are
increasingly becoming unbearable.

A man

could wield every power, but without the power of reason, he is powerless by every reason.

You
can't stay in contact
with your Inner man,
unless you establish
a contract with
your Inner man.

When

you meddle in the affairs of others,

you are bound to get stuck in the middle of every

controversy.

Do not
closet yourself
or else you will waste for the
water closet!

*A man
who analyzes his
motives constantly needs no
motivation,
but one who doesn't
is motivated only by means of
imitation.*

Everyman

has a Life Force

within,

*but the attitude towards this Life
Force differs from*

a everyman.

Rather
than being a force
to be reckoned with,
be reckoned with only by the Force
Within.

Nuances could

be

subtle,

but

stupidity

has

no

subtlety.

Ironing

out differences doesn't

require a

heated appliance, rather,

a cool head

is the

only

appliance

required.

Self-examination minimizes

errors,

but the

lack of self-examination

is an error

in

itself.

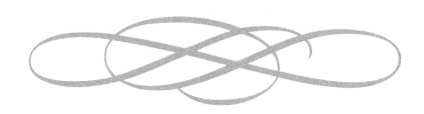

The

best

way to

deal with

your tears

is to

deal with

your

grief.

Friendship
developed during happier times
last but a moment,
but friendship in times of adversity
last a
lifetime.

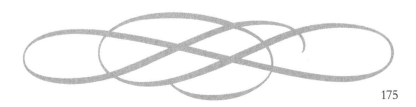

Choices
made for the short run,
results in nothing
but pain in the long
run.

To

overcome hate,

mankind must undergo

nurturing

all

over.

The espousal
of love is not a singular
project for one man,
rather the espousal of love
is a project
for all
men.

Cooling

off does

not keep

one's head

cool;

cooling

down

does.

A
man devoid
of emotion is nothing but
a void
in
motion.

It is
healthy to give in
to tears because
of
grief,
but it is unhealthy
to give in to
grief indefinitely.

Pour out not wickedness

unto the poor,

instead,

let your heart outpour kindness

unto the

poor.

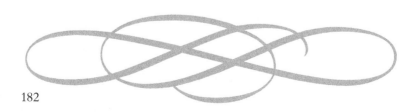

Unless man
recognizes himself in another,
man would forever remain
alienated
from his
fellowman.

Since

time immemorial,

moral

strength remains

the single most arduous

test ever

to face

man.

There would

be the greatest

peace on

Earth if

man would work not to expose the
flaws of his fellow man but

rather his

strengths.

Man
might live by several principles,
but Godly Principles
are the only
ones that assures life.

A man

whose sole focus

is himself detaches no one from himself but his Soul.

Instead

of

wrapping yourself

with ego

put

your

ego

under

wraps!

*Do not slur
if you wish to
glare!*

Working out doesn't work out
challenges;

hard work does.

*If you
don't give up,
chances are that
you won't
give
in.*

Standing firm is

a good thing, but remaining firm is even better.

Since

creation,

ego remains

the single most

divisive trait ever

to

confront

mankind.

Since

ages,

the only

bad influence

that has militated against

man's progress is

man

himself.

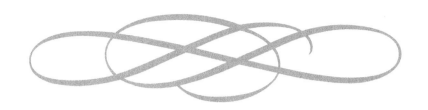

If contentment were beverage,
many will drink.

Any man

who

mocks at

the calamity of others inevitably
drinks from the cup of calamity.

You

are not

*worthy of friendship if you choose
when to be considerate*

and when not to be.

*When a
man perverts the
ways of judgment,
he paves
the way
for his
own misjudgment.*

If the
Pathway of life was a
street,
many would walk.

A man
should only
rise
above his
fellowman
if and only if his
fellowman isn't
beneath
him!

Quickening to

pass

sentence

quickens

one's own judgment.

The countenance
of a man is
like the light of day;
it dims
when it's harboring evil,
and brightens with
good intentions.

A man who

expresses his feelings has a balanced outlook,

but one who suppresses his feelings

has no

balance

whatsoever!

Any man who
recognizes his limitations
has room for progress,
but one who doesn't
retrogresses
without
limit.

Asking

for help when there is the need to do so is

a sign of maturity,

refusing

is

stupidity

at its

apogee.

When

a

man amply exhibits

fellow feeling, the essence

of humanity

is

amplified.

When

a man

exhibits favor

to his fellowman,

he

exhibits

the flavor

in

humanity.

Man is like a flavor
to the soul when
he exhibits favor to another.

The

greatest experiment

yet to be conducted by man is the conduct

between men.

If
liberation is wisdom,
freedom
would rule
every
kingdom.

A man who
alters his tongue
is never worthy
before
the
alter.

*A man
who peaks
into the
affairs of others
only finds trouble
at its
peak.*

Life

is nothing

but a skillful

balance between

joy and

pain.

Wrong
committed in a moment
of weakness is pardonable,
but one committed with
momentum
deserves no
pardon.

There
would be no need for
the law
if mankind would no longer
show cruelty to
another.

*Always
pray for your
actions so you
don't pay for
them.*

The

condition

of the human

family

is based on one condition; the condition

of the

human

mind.

Until

man

bids farewell to cruelty,

cruelty

would

forever

impede

man's

welfare.

It is

humane

to be

mindful

of each

other than

to be mindless

of one

another.

*A man
who works to belittle
others
is
himself belittled,
little
by
little.*

The
capacity
to appreciate beauty
is an
asset, but
the capacity
for destruction is a
liability.

Though the
Earth is adorned
with a marvelous
array of creatures,
the only creature that enriches a
man's life is
man himself.

True

love is

not only

a deep

affection;

true

love

is a

deep

affliction.

Though

man

makes the best company,

cruelty

makes

man

the

worst companion.

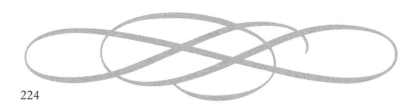

Until

man

learns to embrace

his fellowman, strife

would

continue to

embrace

everyman.

Genuine
remorse is expressed
not by word of mouth,
rather
genuine remorse is
expressed in the
heart.

Life's

most gross inequity

is when

inflicted with pain by

someone

you

trust the most.

There is
nothing like accurate
knowledge but
the
Truth!

Man's
dominant quality is
not to dominate his
fellowman, instead,
man's dominant
quality is to be dominated by that
which Dwells
Within.

When an
individual craves for defiling
habits,
he defies the very
habitat of that which
Dwells
in him.

The

universe is awesome

in nature but the awesomeness

of that which Dwells Within is

incomparable by far.

*A person's
character is
summarized not in his speech:
a person's character is
summarized in his word.*

The
essence of man is
not to progress in life,
the essence of man is to progress
beyond life.

If
making up resolves
every concern,
men
would parade the
streets
wearing makeup.

The

increase

in

lawlessness

is the

result

of the rise

in

selfishness.

The
ability to
love is a gift of light,
but hate originates from the dark.

When

an individual extend a hand in friendship,

love is manifest, but turmoil results when the hand

turns against

the other.

The scope
of a man's promise
is not
by word of mouth, rather the scope of
a man's
promise lies in his
willingness to do so.

*Ever found
your love cooling
down?
Consider cooling
off!*

When

you run

to attain

your goals, you run

to

ruin

your

goals.

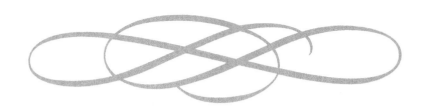

The inordinate

love of riches is caused by nothing
but the inordinate nature of man.

A

man with

no self

control

is a

man

out

of

control.

Hypocrisy

is

a disease

by choice.

To be
inhabited
with envy is one thing and
cohabiting with
one quite another.

The widespread lack of goodness

is caused

by a

widespread

lack

of

goodwill.

*If you
are never open
to any agreement,
you can never get
close to any
achievement.*

Excessive

love of

pleasure

is not only unpleasant,

it is

an

eyesore

in the

extreme.

*Genuine
humility
is uprightness,
but pretentiousness
is a character
flaw.*

The
excessive love for oneself is
caused by an
excessive
lack of concern
for one
another.

An inconsiderate
person is nothing
but a selfish individual,
but a compassionate person
is worthy of
honor.

Lack of
affection
is caused
by
lack of
good
intentions.

Strive

not the path of

least resistance, instead seek

the pathway

of

selfless existence.

Humility

is a

sign of

selfless manifestation, but

arrogance

is nothing but a

selfish

manifestation.

*If
your life
lacks a unified
direction,
try harmonize
your values with
your goals.*

It is
one thing hearing,
and heeding
quite
another.

Can you
make time for
things that matter?
If you can,
you are heading in
the right direction,
if you can't....

What

makes us

good or evil?

Conscience?

Choosing
between good and evil is
hard, but declining to
choose is
easy.

Uprightness is
the compelling force to do what is
right, but

wickedness is the

voluntary choice

to go against what

is right.

Infidelity
is like taking a
beautiful gift from
a loved one and
using it as a
doormat.

*We are
compatible not
because of our values;
we are compatible
because of our
nature.*

Strength of
character is like
a flame; it burns
on the inside, but glows
outwardly.

*It
doesn't
hurt to ask but it
does when you
don't!*

In order
to make time to
know what things matters,
you need to make time
to know what those
things
are.

Unless man

grasp everything there is to know, man would gasp even at the unknown!

Everyone

is honest at some point,

some even most of the time,

but striving to be honest

all the time is the most

honest thing

do.

Looking
outward does
not enhance one's
outlook; looking
inward
does.

To forgive
is a thing of
beauty, but to be
otherwise is ugly,
even
repulsive!

True
love isn't
domiciled in the mind:
true love is
domiciled in the
heart.

A person

with weak conscience

is like damaged goods undesired by many.

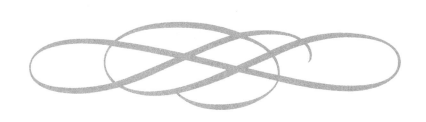

There is

honor in doing

the will of others than others
forcibly doing your

will.

Though a man's

heart is tailor-made for his benefit, the contents of his heart is anything but beneficial.

A man's

mind is like a powerful engine
effective only when it is

controlled.

Instead
of laying claim
for your behavior,
lay clear ground rules for your
behavior.

The

topmost

duty for every

man is to earn the utmost respect

from his

fellowman.

If you

give in to improper

desires, your fruits can never be desired.

At times
loneliness could
be overwhelming,
but at times loneliness
could be an opportunity for self-
examination.

If you
throw aside moral
restraints,
trouble would
follow you
unrestrained.

Marriage

is a permanent

bond broken only when it is traded
off like bonds.

*A man's
wisdom last a day, but
Divine
wisdom last a
lifetime.*

Meditation

*is the link between man and his
Creator, but the link between man
and his fellowman is*

man himself.

The traditions

of men may be antiquated with time, but the tradition of the living God remains anew every day.

The mind

may be an instrument for character development, but the heart still remains the only tool in shaping a person's character.

When we

cultivate reasonableness, we do not expect too much of ourselves, but when we expect too much of ourselves, we lose all

reasonableness.

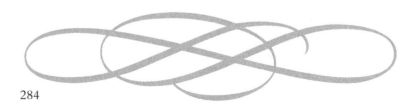

A good
conscience is like
a soft pillow, but a contrary one is
like a drone;
it can only destroy.

Seek not to be praised; rather exult that which is Within!

*The collapse
of social values creates
lawlessness, but the rise in
immorality leads to destruction.*

A critical

heart is not only harmful in nature; a critical heart is appalling in every way.

The wise

understands the need for prudence,
but naivete is the option of

the fool.

God's absolute

perfection is not a standard for humanity rather, God's absolute perfection is a goal towards

perfection.

True courage

*is determined not by one's conquest
of his enemies; true courage is
determined by one's ability to
withstand temptation.*

Though

humanity is a race of intelligent people, man's struggles has always been a race.

The gift of freewill is the epitome of perfection yet man's abuse of this gift renders him imperfect.

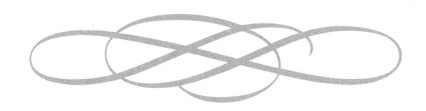

Unless

humanity cultivates the virtues of love and compassion, posterity would be no better!

Subjects

enthrone rulers, but a ruler with no regard for his subjects is a subject of ridicule.

When you

bow before others, others would
bow before you, but when you
refuse to bow, your brow becomes

your bow.

As the

wise feeds on knowledge, the fool feeds on gossip.

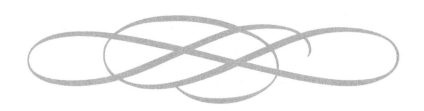

Revenge

*is like hard earned revenue paid
only in the reverse!*

It is like a

smack in one's own face when one's sacrifices goes

unappreciated.

Consolation
is like a dish enjoyed
only by the
crushed.

Works

accomplished with

*purity are revered for a life time,
but those accomplished with
arrogance suffers a lifetime*

of resentment.

Heartache

is repaired not by work tools;
heartache is repaired by the tools
that resides only in

the heart.

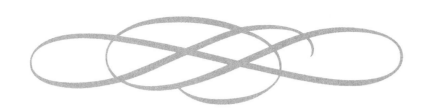

A man

with fragile emotions is like a
feather in motion.

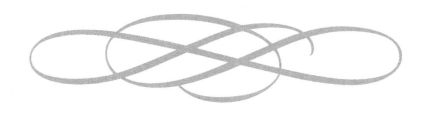

The process

of rationalization is the only
instrument capable of measuring
the depth of one's wisdom.

A crumb

served with love is better than a sumptuous meal served

with contempt!

Life is

not about putting people to the test; life is about being up to

the test.

If you

are fortunate to breeze through life, spare a thought for those who are bruising through

life.

The purpose

of seeking enlightenment is for spiritual nourishment, any other purpose is

malnutrition.

God diversified

wisdom among all men so
knowledge of him would unify all

men.

If riches

were everlasting, bankruptcy
would have a different meaning.

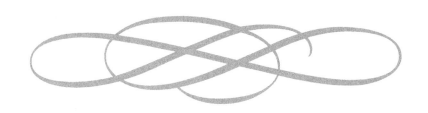

As the

face of the Lord shines on the believer, so does the face of the believer glows in

the Lord.

Imagination

is like journeying through time in a specialized vessel; you!

There is

blessing in getting accustomed with the things of the Lord than customizing the things of

the world.

If wisdom

were imbibed only to intellectuals,
the unlettered should have been
extinct.

Though

God is supreme beyond imagination, His essence is revealed to humanity in humility.

Man might

go to the ends of the earth in search of peace, but that which provides peace dwells within.

Setting your goals beyond
your reach, only breaches
your capabilities.

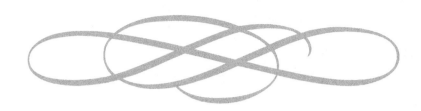

Feasting

doesn't make one spiritual; fasting does.

Honesty
is like a flower that never
withers.

The

bedrock of humanity is true friendship.

Do you

esteem your friends as highly as yourself? If you don't then you are no friend.

Notes

does not connect people,
conversation does.

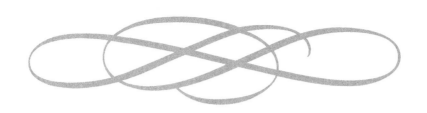

Transgression

is like the use of a credit card;
commit now, pay later.

Airing

your weaknesses could help chart your life unerringly.

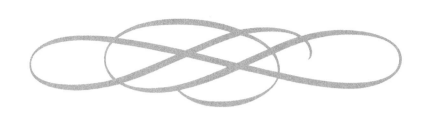

Tendency

to wary is tendency to

worry.

Absorb

wisdom like a sponge absorbing water, and you will flow like a river nurturing fertile

grounds.

Plucking

one's eardrums does not stop a tantrum, freeing them does.

An evil

thought is like a great atomic missile: its design awesome, its impact devastating.

Figuring

out the complexities of life is like figuring out the complexity of the mind.

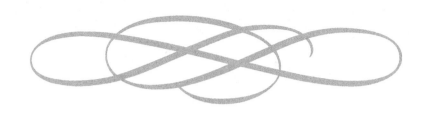

Unquestionable obedience is loyalty unequaled.

If life

was caused by some great cosmic accident, no man should ever take credit for his

intelligence.

A word

of hope is like the seed of an oak tree: it can blossom beyond

expectation.

It is

better to be a discerning observer
than a dissenting

one.

To test a

spouse's affection, pretend falling off a cliff and watch for his or her reaction.

Do not

be thrilled by the things of this world, instead be thrilled by the Maker of this world.

To attain

a life of balance, one needs to balance spiritual and material pursuits evenly.

An air

of superiority is a sign of imperfection: the spirit of humility paves the way to

perfection.

It is an

undeniable fact that love and hate remains the two most dominant opposing forces since creation.

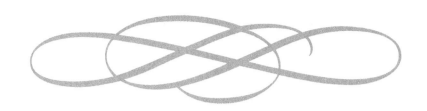

Diligence

is the fruit of wisdom, but
ineptitude is the seed of laxity.

Excellence

is never attained by fickle minds; excellence is attained by fishing minds.

Arrogance

toward the general good is acceptable, but arrogance toward one's self is despicable.

A humble

heart is a heart of understanding, but an arrogant heart is a heart of confusion.

Stray

not into the congregation of fools, instead seek for the company of the

wise.

If insight

was endowed to creatures with the largest eyeballs, owls would be counselors.

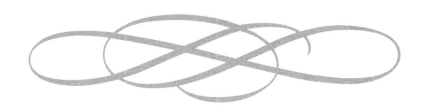

Fair

mindedness is dignifying, but a prejudiced mind radiates

disdain.

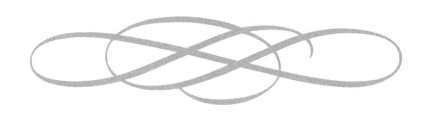

Nobility
has no wings, but soars like
a bird.

A person

who lives in sin can't flee from evil, rather, a person who lives in sin is pursued by evil.

A prudent man feels the need only to feed his soul, but a glutton fills his belly needlessly.

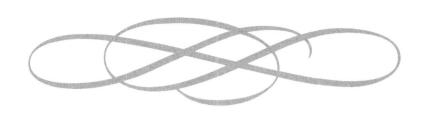

It is safer

to encounter a neighbor's wickedness than to cherish a stranger's

advances.

Honesty

is a way of life, but honor is a crown for life.

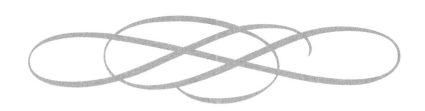

Temptation
is a test that can never be put to
rest.

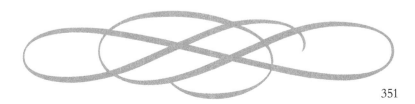

See

your core values as your chore responsibility and everything will be just fine.

If the

ransom for a man's life were his wealth, the poor would be sold for

ransom.

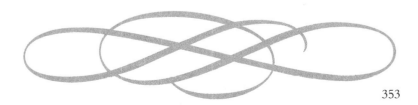

A man

who is well prepared can well perform his tasks, but a man who is ill-prepared see preparation even

as a task!

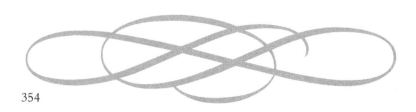

Limited

abilities means limited means, but unlimited means, means unlimited abilities.

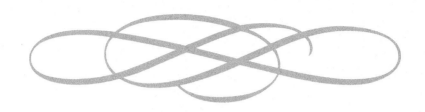

Noble

birth does not make a man noble,
noble life does.

*If you
can't put a lid on your mouth, your
lip could be tampered
with.*

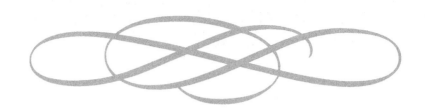

An

alcoholic can only refrain if he turns a workaholic.

Ever

wondered why you suffer setbacks? Consider stepping

back.

If
you want your life to be straight,
strive to stay on a straight

course.

It is one

thing daydreaming, and dreaming
during the day quite

another.

If

your life is full of airs, your era would be full of

errors.

*If you
are hard to deal with, you are
probably hard of hearing.*

Willpower

is like an aroma smelled only by one's self.

Curiosity

is like the beauty of a strange woman; it draws you, but at

a price.

The depth

of a person's love is measured by
the breadth of his deeds.

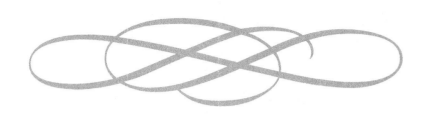

To be

charitable is to ensure the essence of life.

Wisdom
is like a dish enjoyed only by
a minority.

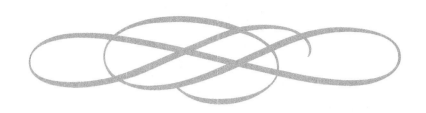

True

*love is like a lamp that glows
unceasingly.*

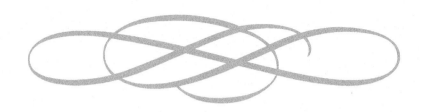

A man's

strength resides not in his muscles
but in his heart.

To donate

your priceless possession

is to pass the test of willpower.

The warm-hearted

imputes good motives, but for
the cold-hearted, bad motives is a
motivation.

Men may

be memorialized for their accomplishments, but the accomplishments of that which Dwells Within is

eternal.

A clean appearance may be dignifying, but a clean heart reflects His Holiness.

Always

be inclined towards wisdom and let reason be your

voice.

Decisiveness

is a sign of courage, but indecision
is discouragement without

a doubt.

A friend's
success is a cause for celebration
not suspicion.

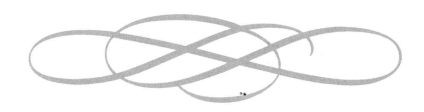

If you
think you succeeded on your own,
attain your next achievement
without breathing and see if you
will succeed.

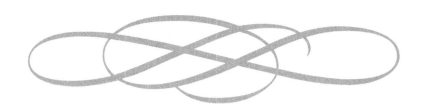

It is

honorable to exude power than to exert power.

If you can't visualize your goals, you can't actualize your

dreams.

It is hard

to bear anything in mind especially when you care less about your mindlessness.

It is

better to be counted on than to count for absolutely

nothing.

To be

able to face the future, one has to embrace his or her very

nature.

If you

gloat over the difficulties of others,
others would bloat your

difficulties.

It is

better for a man to be plundered for his wealth than to have his soul plunged.

The function

of the heart is not to invigorate the stream of life, but rather, the function of the heart is to retain that which invigorates

the Soul.

The wise

takes pleasure in the fruit of his labor, but the fool revels in the generosity of the wise.

If wealth guarantees love, those with little means would search for love and never find it.

Suspense

is like an invincible prison with no need for latches nor

locks.

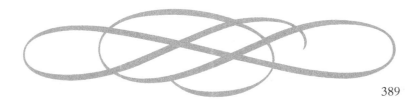

Foolishness

is like a cloak best displayed only in public.

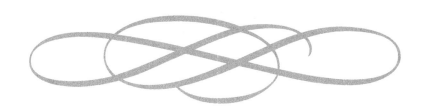

A man

who could hardly forgive could hardly be a neighbor.

Rash decisions would only rush you through life. Be rational and you will enjoy life to the full.

If
you don't sugarcoat your words,
you will gain respect wherever

you go.

Moral

weakness is a vulnerability, but
sound judgment is a quality desired
by many.

The wise

imitates the upright, but the fool takes pride in his folly.

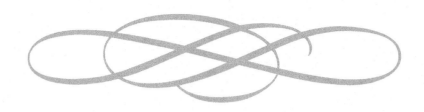

It is

*better to be endowed with the gift
of discernment than to be adorned
with gifts.*

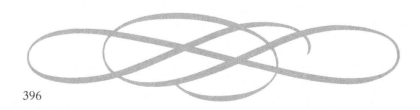

Embracing

a promiscuous woman in your
bosom only makes you a ransom

for her pleasures.

A virtuous woman is like a gem, but an adulterous woman is like a germ.

A man

who quenches the thirst of another
fills the well of his own

soul.

Deceit

is like a self-inflicted wound; it hurts no other person than one's own

self.

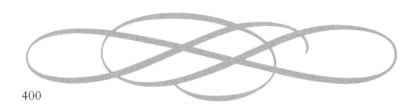

A gracious person is admired by all, but one full of arrogance is the scorn of all.

The world

might envy the wealthy and the famous, but the meek and the gentle, the world

adores.

No matter

how renowned a man might be, his life is invincible unless he is well-known by that which Dwells

within.

Self-righteousness is nothing but self-indulgence.

In everything,

let your reasonableness justify the reason why you were

created.

Humility

doesn't impute lack of achievement; humility is an achievement only a few can

attain.

It is

unquestionable that love conquers all, but to conquer under the pretence of

love is highly questionable.

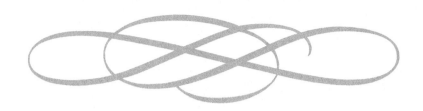

Contemplating

the vastness of the universe is a humbling experience, but knowing the Creator of the universe is an incomparable experience.

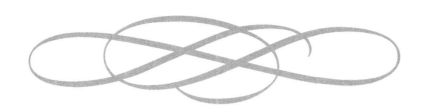

A man

who opens his doors to others
hardly finds closed doors.

If

simplicity were inferior, nobility would be ascribed only to the flamboyant.

Until

man identifies with one another,
equality would forever remain a

dream.

A man

who holds others in low estimation is revered only in the estimation of fools.

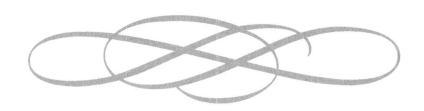

Ignoring facts

contemptibly confirms only one fact: Ignorance.

Exhibition

of power is justified only when it inspires hope and not

fear.

Unless

*men halts leveling suspicion
against each other, life would
never be a level playing field.*

Sharing

in the celebration of others is the best celebration the world could ever have.

Character

development is not what you know; character development is the proof of what you know.

It is one thing taken offense by something, and sitting on the fence quite another.

If you
are accelerating through life, you
are probably not celebrating

life.

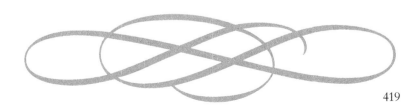

Subjecting

one to ridicule has only one benefit;
spite!

The human

body is not a mere mechanism of blood and tissue; the human body is an extra-ordinary engineering beyond every mechanism.

Instead

of looking down on others, let others look up to

you.

Returning

evil with evil gains nothing in return; turning away from evil reaps blessings in good

returns.

A sincere

man is very easy to approach, but insincerity incurs reproach

easily.

Though

man is an amazing creature,
his relationship with another is
anything but

amazing.

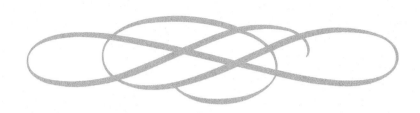

Commonsense

*is the only virtue that distinguishes
between the wise and the not*

so wise.

The purpose

of mobilization mainly is to establish a purpose.

Life
is not worth living because of wealth;
life is worth living because of
self-worth.

The world

could be one big nation if only it could be guided with only one big notion; the notion of love.

Believing

anything that pleases the eye could have only one consequence; a life beyond belief.

Envisioning

with the eyes offers no insight,
envisioning with the heart

does.

Misleading
others is not leadership;
showing is.

Cultivating

the culture of tolerance is the best culture for the world

today.

All men

are equal, save the heart.

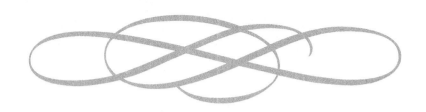

A true

*worshiper isn't one who worships
the Creator; true worshiper is one
who has the favor of the Creator.*

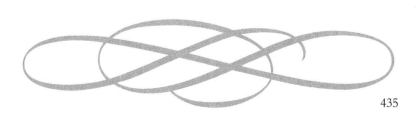

Taking

delight in flattery is like a blind taking delight in

daylight.

*The best
way to be on guard
is letting that which dwells in
you be your
safeguard.*

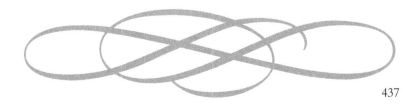

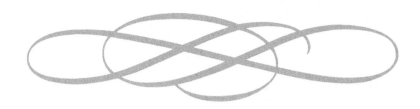

Co-existence was the reason man was endowed with reason.

Disparaging

remark doesn't hurt; disparaging remark is hate.

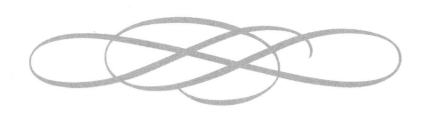

Nobility

is not by appearance; nobility is by perception.

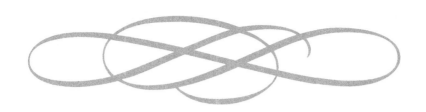

Compassion
towards all is empathy for
all.

Vexation in the heart is an infestation of the heart.

*The
rod does not only punish, it teaches
as well.*

There

*is no criticism difficult to accept
than the truth about*

oneself.

*Emancipating
one's mind brings peace to
oneself.*

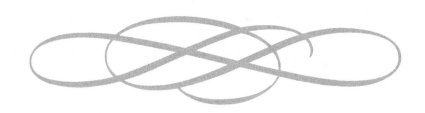

Inculcating

love to another is the most cherished lesson of all lessons.

Man

is a complexity bundled up in one body yet man's nature is simplicity open to all.

A careful

observer is a thoughtful person,
but a thoughtless person don't

give a damn.

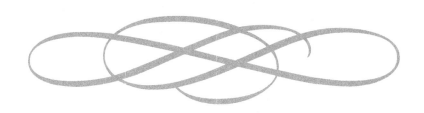

*The coldest
place is not out there; the coldest
place is within.*

Raging

affection is nothing but
promiscuity on the rampage.

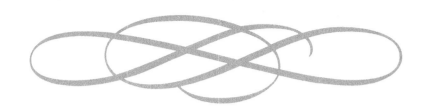

It is

one thing being immune to criticism, and being inundated with criticisms quite another.

A man's

true nature is like a molecule; it requires special equipment to

detect.

Fragile

emotion is resentment in

motion.

Being

tenderly compassionate is saintly, but being bitterly angry could be deadly.

Being attentive to

the commandments is better than
striving to command attention.

Being

humble is not foolishness, being
humble is noble.

Nobility

is the seed for promotion, but demotion is the fruit of

arrogance.

The

value of the rich might be his
wealth, but the value of the
humble lies in his humility.

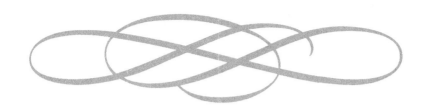

Man

might be dynamic in his pursuits,
but the attributes of dynamism is
never his making.

Rules

are made not for subversion : rules are made so man might live in submission.

If arrogance

is fearlessness, men of courage
would be the most

dishonored.

461

A man

can shrug of his critics, but he cannot shed off his

criticisms.

One

needs to be guided or else one would be

misguided.

The heart

of man defines his character,
but the definition of the mind is
anything but mind boggling.

If you are

fun of treachery, you will be
fanned by treachery.

If you
stand in the way of others, others
will stay in your

way.

If man

were an abstract being, his thoughts would have remained in his head forever.

During

unstable times, man might rely on economic and other indicators to foretell the future, but the key to the future is really held by that which abides within us.

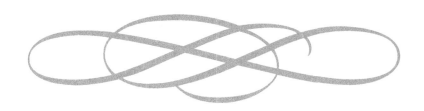

Gross

insubordination does not only occur in official circles; gross insubordination exist even in our relationship with the Creator.

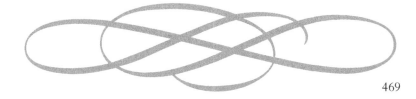

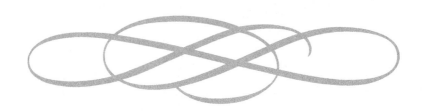

Faith

untested is hope abandoned.

Instead

of adopting the things of this world, be adept with the things of the world.

Assigning

a task to one is a reminder that
mankind is himself a task onto

himself.

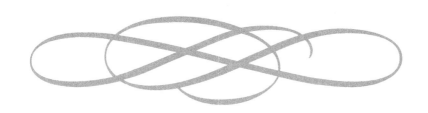

Yearn

*not the respect of others, rather,
earn the respect of others.*

It is one thing

being obedient, and being
dishonest quite another.

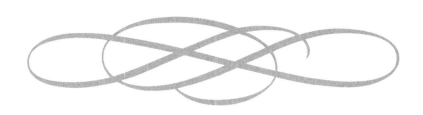

When you resist temptation, you are doing nothing but insisting on your salvation.

When

you immerse yourself in humility,
your impact on humanity is
anything but immense.

*If you
give in to doubt, doubt would give
you away.*

It takes

substance to sustain oneself, but it takes far more than substance to sustain one's life.

When you

clean up your act, it is for a moment, but when you clean up your life it is for eternity.

Failing

to take action can only result in one action; getting kicked to take

one.

Having

a moderate estimation of your abilities is called modesty; having the opposite is called

ignorance.

Trust
is like a pay check; it must be
earned.

Acknowledging
one's limitation is not a weakness;
refusing to acknowledge is.

The

complexity of nature is not mind boggling; the complexity of nature is mind blowing.

Nature's

complexity lies not in its diversity;
nature's complexity lies with
humanity.

A heartfelt

gift is like a key; it opens the door to the heart.

A good

thought is a nourishment to the mind, but an evil one is a

malnutrition.

You don't

drink spirit to be in high spirits:
you spare to be in good

spirits.

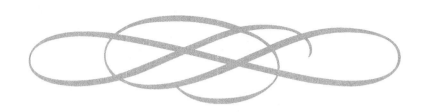

Aside the dead, no man is dead to compassion.

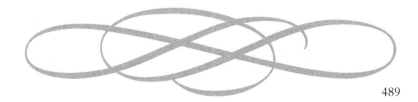

Life is

shaped by special moments;
especially those that come
unannounced.

The funeral
of the cruel is a jubilation, but that
of the upright is a

celebration.

*A life
of hallmarks are landmarks for
posterity.*

Deceit

is like a disease that infects only the willing.

A family

with no structures is like a house full of

fractures.

*If the
dead could aid the living, the living
would wish to be*

dead.

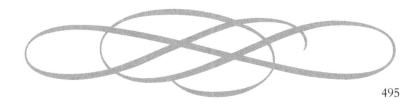

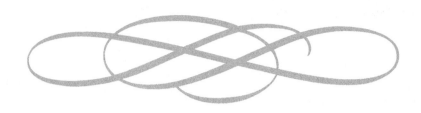

Life is

not about how much you weigh,
life is about how much weight you
can carry.

Wisdom is the backbone of the upright, but the backbone of the fool is the whip.

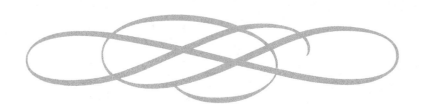

Perfection

is like a shadow; the closer you draw, the farther it drifts.

There would

be the greatest fulfillment in the world if in each individual, man would exploit not his deepest of fears but his highest of hopes.

When it

is in your capacity to give, give freely, without equivocation, for it is an investment beyond conventional wisdom.

Substance

with no honor is like a dish with no taste.

Man might formulate the most complex of doctrines to govern the nations, but none is sufficient without the doctrine of love.

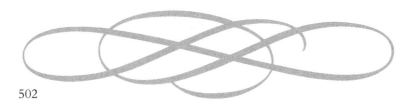

It is not

in a man's interest to show compassion to another, it is for his very survival.

When the Good Lord made the Heavens and the Earth, he had only one thing in mind : You

Innocence

is like an invincible shield: it protects its host in ways

beyond comprehension.

Guilt

is like an awful odor, it roams freely without fear nor favor.

The Lord says, " I will guide you along the best pathway for your life. I will advise you and watch over you. Do not be like a senseless horse or mule that needs a bit and bridle to keep it under control.
Psalm 32: 8-9 NLT

The end.

Reflections from Beyond – Volume 2

Excerpts:

Wisdom loves company, but loves cooperation even better.

You don't take what you don't have if you have what is takes.

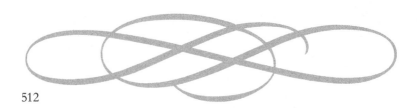

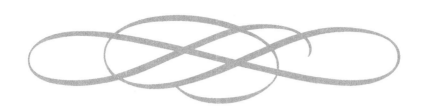

Pretence could be fun if only it had no price.

If you know how you were made, no man born of a woman can unmake you.

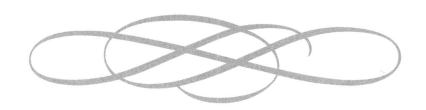

A man who doesn't follow advice can only lead the fool.

-*The Gods Declare* is a suspense filled non-fiction with parallels to real life situations. Publisher's Email: <u>www.Iuniverse.com.</u>

-*Doctor Huu Pham*, the Author's Doctor could be reached at 1048 North Pine Hills Road, Orlando, Florida, 32808. 407 299 3166

-*Midwest Center for Stress and Anxiety*, 106 N Church Street #200, Oak Habor, OH 43449

-*Kwesi Korreh, Attorney and Counselor at Law admitted at Florida and New Jersey.* 6500 West Colonial Dr. Suite C, Orlando, Florida, 32818. 407 580 9966, 862 215 4486. Email: <u>KKorreh@lawoffic-esofkwesikorreh.com</u>

-*Pastors*: Sylvester Athoro, House of Glory Church, 5514 Edgewater Drive, Orlando, Florida, 32810, Bishop Kofi Akotua Obeng, P. O. Box 19883, Accra North, Ghana. Email: <u>OKITIKEI6@YAHOO.COM</u>

<u>Note</u>: Proceeds goes to *Gold Mind Charities,* a not-for-profit organization aimed at empowering among others, persons with severe Anxiety and Panic Disorder, here in Florida, and sub-Sahara Africa where this debilitating condition has no name, virtually. Author Email: <u>degieus@yahoo.com.</u>